MY FAVOURITE HYMNS

My favourite Hymns

CLASSIC HYMNS AND MUSIC FROM THE INSPIRATIONAL ITV SERIES

With an introduction by John Stapleton

GRANADA

My Favourite Hymns is a Granada Television Production

First published in Great Britain in 2001

by Granada Media, an imprint of André Deutsch Limited
20 Mortimer Street
London W1V 5HA

in association with Granada Media Group

Compilation copyright © **Granada Media Group Ltd** 2001

ISBN 0 233 99946 9

Music by the Orgone Company.
Additional musical arrangement by Terry Burrows.

Design by **designsection**, Frome, Somerset

Printed and bound in Italy by Eurolitho

10 9 8 7 6 5 4 3 2 1

MY FAVOURITE HYMNS

CONTENTS

INTRODUCTION

BY JOHN STAPLETON

Y OU DON'T HAVE TO BE A REGULAR CHURCH-GOER to have a favourite hymn. For most of us know many more hymns than we realize, although it might mean casting our minds back to the dim, distant days of childhood, of Sunday School, end-of-term assemblies, Easter services and Harvest festivals. On such occasions even the most cynical schoolboy – one who would habitually mime to the hymns at morning assembly – would launch with gusto into *Onward Christian Soldiers*, *Fight the Good Fight* or *He Who Would Valiant Be*. Without knowing it, he, too, had his favourite hymns.

Hymns often represent our first introduction to real music and, as such, invariably hold a special place in our hearts. They can mean so many different things to different people. Some people like a particular hymn for the tune;

others for the words or sentiments. Hymns can evoke memories of families and friends, work and play, happiness and sadness. They can be uplifting; they can be soothing. They can offer strength in times of doubt, inspiration in times of need, comfort in times of stress. Quite simply, there are hymns to suit every situation.

While presenting the television series *My Favourite Hymns*, I have been struck by the sheer diversity of people – from all walks of life – to whom hymns quite obviously mean so much. Our guests have ranged from the Archbishop of Canterbury to Spike Milligan; from Toyah Wilcox to Mary Whitehouse; from Frank McCourt to Gordon Banks; and from Sir Ranulph Fiennes to Bruce Jones, alias Les Battersby of *Coronation Street* fame. Who would have thought that Les Battersby, who surely would only go near a church in order to pinch the lead off the roof, could be visibly moved by hymns?

This beautiful book captures some of the highlights of the series. Our splendid array of guests not only pick their favourite hymns and give the reasons behind their choices, but they also talk about their faith and their lives with great fortitude and honesty.

Actress Jean Marsh, co-creator of *Upstairs Downstairs*, remembers the loss of a close school friend during the Second World War. Lord Hattersley reveals how he discovered that his late father had been a priest. Author Frank McCourt reflects on the impoverished childhood in Limerick which inspired his best-selling novel, *Angela's Ashes*. The late Dame Barbara Cartland talks about Diana, Princess of Wales. Writer Dr Maya Angelou, the victim of appalling racial bigotry in the Deep South of the United States in the 1930s, discusses her emotional first trip to Africa. Mary Whitehouse tells of how she won over a heckler who had thrown an open can of paint at her. And another *Coronation Street* star, William Roache, describes how seeing the ghost of his baby daughter gave him the strength to cope with her death.

On a lighter note, Ann Widdecombe reveals a surprising past as a practical joker, Frank Carson remembers how at a Royal Variety Performance he made the Queen roar with laughter at an impromptu gag about the royal corgis, and Sir Harry Secombe confesses that, as a young boy, shyness about performing at family gatherings used to force him to belt out *Onward Christian Soldiers* in the seclusion of the toilet... with the door open!

And what of their choices of hymn? For some, like Sir Harry, it brought back amusing childhood memories. For Eric Sykes, who is registered blind, is deaf and has had bypass surgery, *Count Your Blessings* sums up his optimistic philosophy of life. It must be said that he also selected the sea-faring hymn *Eternal Father, Strong to Save* on the grounds that he served with Lord Nelson in a previous life...

A number of guests – among them the Archbishop of Canterbury and actor Edward Woodward – chose hymns which had been sung at their weddings. Others chose their parents' favourite hymns, while Richard Whiteley opted for *O Son of Man* because it brought back poignant memories of his sister's funeral, at which that particular hymn was played.

Lord Hattersley feels close affinities with the socialist hymn *When Will Thou Save the People* and Toyah Wilcox, the former high priestess of punk, enjoys the

rousing *Immortal, Invisible God Only Wise* because it chimes with the image she has of herself as a sort of latter-day Boadicea. Fellow musician Rick Wakeman feels strong ties with *The Day Thou Gavest Lord Has Ended* and reveals that he frequently plays it on the piano at night before going to bed. And TV weather presenter Sian Lloyd says that her idea of heaven is relaxing in a bath with *Amazing Grace* on the CD player.

My sincere thanks go to all of the guests on *My Favourite Hymns* for sharing their thoughts, beliefs and reminiscences. I hope that within these pages you will find something illuminating and edifying, and that someone has chosen your favourite hymn.

John Stapleton, January 2001

THE HYMNS

O PRAISE YE THE LORD · THE PASSION CHORALE · THERE IS A GREEN HILL FAR AWAY
WHEN WILT THOU SAVE THE PEOPLE · ETERNAL FATHER, STRONG TO SAVE
HAIL GLORIOUS SAINT PATRICK · JESUS, TENDER SHEPHERD, HEAR ME
ONWARD CHRISTIAN SOLDIERS · ABIDE WITH ME · AMAZING GRACE
ALL CREATURES OF OUR GOD AND KING · ALL HAIL THE POWER OF JESUS' NAME
ALL PEOPLE THAT ON EARTH DO DWELL · ALL THINGS BRIGHT AND BEAUTIFUL
BE THOU MY VISION · COUNT YOUR BLESSINGS · DEAR LORD AND FATHER OF MANKIND
FAITH OF OUR FATHERS · HE WHO WOULD VALIANT BE · SOUL OF MY SAVIOUR
WHO WOULD TRUE VALOUR SEE JERUSALEM · LOVE DIVINE ALL LOVES EXCELLING
FIGHT THE GOOD FIGHT · GLORIOUS THINGS OF THEE ARE SPOKEN · GO DOWN MOSES
GRACIOUS SPIRIT, HOLY GHOST · HAIL QUEEN OF HEAVEN · SWING LOW SWEET CHARIOT
HOW SWEET THE NAME OF JESUS SOUNDS · IMMORTAL, INVISIBLE GOD ONLY WISE
JESU, LOVER OF MY SOUL · LEAD KINDLY LIGHT · MINE EYES HAVE SEEN THE GLORY
MY SOUL THERE IS A COUNTRY · NOW THANK WE ALL OUR GOD · O SON OF MAN
PRAISE TO THE LORD, THE ALMIGHTY THE KING OF CREATION · PRAISE MY SOUL
THE DAY THOU GAVEST, LORD, IS ENDED · THE KING OF LOVE MY SHEPHERD IS
JESUS' HEART ALL BURNING · THE LORD IS MY SHEPHERD · AVE MARIA

O PRAISE YE THE LORD

'**M**Y WIFE EILEEN WAS MY CHILDHOOD SWEETHEART. She really is a great help to me in so many ways. She's my best friend and I think that at the very heart of every secure marriage is friendship. She doesn't intrude into my professional life, she remains her own person. She often says to people, "I am not a clergy person. I've no desire to be ordained but I want to be an ordinary Christian working out my own discipleship in my own way." And I respect her for it.

'When I took my wife and four children up to run the parish of St Nicholas's, Durham, it was a challenge for us all. It was very tough at times. It was a very cold vicarage with about eight bedrooms and my wife used to hoover the house wearing gloves, double jerseys and so on. But we look back now and see it as a wonderful time, of renewal, of change.

'*O Praise Ye The Lord* is a great hymn of praise that was sung at our wedding. We have it sung at every baptism of our children, our children have it as their wedding hymn, and it will be sung at my funeral service… although I hope that won't be for a long time to come. It's been one of those great hymns that have punctuated our ministry together.'

Dr George Carey, Archbishop of Canterbury

O Praise ye the Lord!
  praise him in the height;
rejoice in his word, ye angels of light;
ye heavens, adore him,
  by whom ye were made,
and worship before him,
  in brightness arrayed.

O praise ye the Lord!
  praise him upon the earth,
in tuneful accord, ye sons of new birth;
praise him who hath brought you
  his grace from above,
praise him who hath taught you
  to sing of his love.

O praise ye the Lord!
  all things that give sound;
each jubilant chord re-echo around;
  loud organs his glory
forth tell in deep tone,
and, sweet harp, the story
of what he hath done.

O praise ye the Lord!
  thanksgiving and song
to him be outpoured all ages along:
for love in creation,
for heaven restored,
for grace of salvation,
O praise ye the Lord!

THE PASSION CHORALE

O sacred head sore wounded,
Defiled and put to scorn;
O kingly head surrounded
With mocking crown of thorn:
What sorrow mars thy grandeur?
Can death thy bloom deflower?
O countenance whose splendour
The hosts of heaven adore.

Thy beauty, long-desired,
Hath vanished from our sight;
Thy power is all expired,
And quenched the light of light
Ah me! For whom thou diest,
Hide not so far thy grace:
Show me, O love most highest,
The brightness of thy face.

JEAN MARSH, THE CO-CREATOR OF *UPSTAIRS DOWNSTAIRS*,
in which she played parlourmaid Rose, surprised – and alarmed –
her parents by converting to Catholicism.

'Converting to Catholicism was a great way of rebelling. My father was
very extreme, very left wing. He was quite a serious Communist who
used to talk about churches and cathedrals and say they all ought to be
pulled down and turned into workers' flats. When we went to school, my
sister and I were supposed not to sing in assembly, but we both did.

'Listening to hymns then I always had a sense that there was a guardian
angel, somebody watching over me. I got that sense from my friend who sat
next to me at school. One day there was a terrible air-raid and she and her
whole family were killed. I went to school the next day and they announced
that she was dead, but I had guessed anyway from the empty seat. I had a
feeling then not just of sadness but of a sense of fortune, of a hand on my
shoulder, and since then I have felt that hand on my shoulder from time to
time. I do feel that I have been saved from a number of dangerous situations.

'I love the language of *Passion Chorale*. It's got such vigorous words, it's almost
like Oaths. And Bach is one of my favourite composers – he's very consistent.'

Jean Marsh

THERE IS A GREEN HILL FAR AWAY

There is a green hill far away,
without a city wall,
where the dear Lord was crucified
who died to save us all.

We may not know, we cannot tell,
what pains he had to bear,
but we believe it was for us
he hung and suffered there.

He died that we might be forgiv'n,
he died to make us good;
that we might go at last to heav'n,
saved by his precious blood.

There was no other good enough
to pay the price of sin;
he could only unlock the gate
of heav'n, and let us in.

O dearly, dearly has he loved,
and we must love him too,
and trust in his redeeming blood,
and try his works to do.

'THERE IS A GROSS LACK OF WHAT I CALL meaningful Easter thanksgiving music, for what Jesus did for our life, but *There is a Green Hill Far Away* is perhaps the one that personifies the best of Easter music. It is a most beautiful tune with lovely words and accomplishes really what a hymn should be, which is tell the story as it is in a beautiful way so that by the end of it you just go, "Thank you very much."'

Rick Wakeman

'I USED TO GO AND VISIT MY GRANDMOTHER'S GRAVE and quite near the cemetery was a big mound. I used to think of that as the hill and I could always imagine Jesus on a similar-looking hill. Whenever I saw it, that was the hymn that came back into my mind.'

Dame Vera Lynn

THERE IS A GREEN HILL FAR AWAY

WHEN WILT THOU SAVE THE PEOPLE

When wilt thou save the people?
O God of mercy, when?
The people, Lord, the people,
Not thrones and crowns, but men!
Flowers of thy heart, O God, are they;
Let them not pass like weeds away,
Their heritage a sunless day:
God save the people!

Shall crime bring crime for ever,
Strength aiding still the strong?
Is it thy will, O Father,
That man shall toil for wrong?

'No,' say thy mountains; 'No,' thy skies;
Man's clouded sun shall brightly rise,
And songs be heard instead of sighs:
God save the people!

When wilt thou save the people?
O God of mercy, when?
The people, Lord, the people,
Not thrones and crowns, but men!
God save the people; thine they are,
Thy children, as thy angels fair;
From vice, oppression, and despair
God save the people!

THE FORMER DEPUTY LEADER OF THE LABOUR PARTY explains how his Sheffield upbringing influenced his socialist and religious indoctrination.

'As well as going to church, which we did almost every Sunday morning, we used to go to the old cobbler's shop of the Brightside and Carbrook Co-operative Society. And in the old cobbler's shop we were told about the religious implications of socialism, or the socialist implications of religion. I believed then, as I believe now, that a God who looks after the humble and meek can be associated with the socialist ethic. It was always those parts of the Bible which conformed to our view of society that were read. There were sermons about greater equality and always about pulling down the rich and the prosperous. And there were some exclusively socialist hymns.

'When Will Thou Save The People is a hymn from socialist Sunday School. It not only has a great rousing tune, but the words are pretty radical because it describes the people who God ought not to save: "The people, Lord, the people, not thrones and crowns, but men."'

Lord Roy Hattersley

ETERNAL FATHER, STRONG TO SAVE

Eternal Father, strong to save,
whose arm doth bind the restless wave,
who bidd'st the mighty ocean deep
its own appointed limits keep:
O hear us when we cry to thee
for those in peril on the sea.

O Saviour, whose almighty word
the winds and waves submissive heard,
who walkedst on the foaming deep,
and calm, amid its rage, didst sleep:
O hear us when we cry to thee
for those in peril on the sea.

O sacred Spirit, who didst brood
upon the waters dark and rude,
and bid their angry tumult cease,
and give, for wild confusion, peace:
O hear us when we cry to thee
for those in peril on the sea.

O Trinity of love and pow'r,
our brethren shield in danger's hour.
From rock and tempest fire and foe,
protect them whereso'er they go,
and ever let them rise to thee
glad hymns of praise from land and sea.

'MY PARENTS ALWAYS SAY I WAS a remarkably difficult child. I was terribly defiant, terribly rude, I used to play the most awful tricks on people. My father was in what was then known as the Admiralty and we travelled around a great deal during my childhood. When we went to Singapore we had some Chinese staff to look after us, and the house boy always left his slippers at the bottom of a huge flight of steps that went up to our house. Those slippers were a perpetual temptation to me, and I always used to hide them. It didn't matter what punishment I received, I always used to hide them.

'This hymn is a direct connection with my childhood, which was obviously very based around the navy. When my father died last year, this was the central hymn at his memorial service.'

Rt. Hon. Ann Widdecombe, MP

ETERNAL FATHER, STRONG TO SAVE

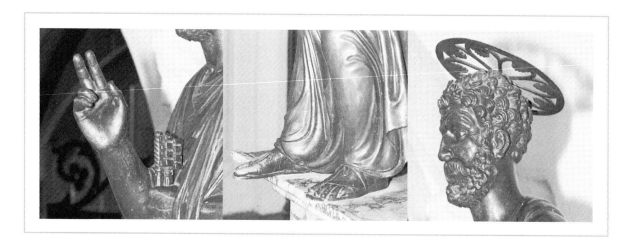

'THIS HYMN IS FOR THOSE IN PERIL ON THE SEA. I think in a previous life I served with Nelson. It might not have been Nelson, because I might have been a Spaniard then! But I've got that feeling. I've always loved the sea.'

Eric Sykes

'THE ISLANDS ARE A VERY IMPORTANT PART OF MY LIFE. I represent the Isle of Skye and enjoy sailing as much as I possibly can. You get a whole different perspective of the coastline when you see it from the sea rather than when you approach it by road. And, of course, the fishing industry is very important traditionally in the north of Scotland. This hymn has really good sentiments that remind me of that sense of island community which I think is so vital.'

Rt. Hon. Charles Kennedy, MP

HAIL GLORIOUS SAINT PATRICK

'**T**HIS IS A VERY JOYFUL HYMN, but I have mixed feelings about Saint Patrick. I think he should have left Ireland alone – we were doing all right before Catholicism came.

'Unless you grow up as a Catholic, or as an Irish Catholic, you'll never understand the power of the Church. They get you early and train you to have a sense of sin. When I was teaching later in New York, I had very bright adolescents and we got to James Joyce's *Portrait of the Artist*, to the sermon on hell, and damnation and guilt. I noticed these kids, many of them Jewish or Protestant or nothing, and they looked blank. I said: "You don't understand, do you? You don't know what the seven deadly sins are, do you? If you don't know the seven deadly sins, how can you enjoy yourself?"

'So there were the seven deadly sins and the ten commandments and then various sins in Limerick that nobody ever heard of because there was something called the unforgivable sin. You'd say to a priest: "What is the unforgivable sin?" He'd reply: "Nobody knows." "How do you know if you've committed it?" "You'll know. No priest can forgive it."

'But this is a hymn that I like anyway. It should be a national anthem.'

Frank McCourt

Hail, glorious Saint Patrick,
  dear saint of our
Isle, on us thy poor children
  bestow a sweet
Smile; and now thou art high
  in the mansions
Above, on Erin's green valleys
  look down in
Thy love. On Erin's green valleys,
  on Erin's
Green valleys,
  on Erin's green valleys look
Down in thy love.

Ever bless and defend the sweet
  land of our
Birth, where the shamrock still blooms as
When thou wert on earth,
  and our hearts shall
Yet burn, wheresoever we roam,
For God and Saint Patrick,
  and our native
Home. For God and Saint Patrick,
  for God
And Saint Patrick, For God
  and Saint Patrick,
And our native home.

HAIL GLORIOUS SAINT PATRICK

JESUS, TENDER SHEPHERD, HEAR ME

Jesus, tender shepherd, hear me,
Bless thy little lamb tonight;
Through the darkness be thou near me;
Watch my sleep till morning light.

All this day thy hand has led me
And I thank thee for thy care;
Thou hast clothed me, warmed and fed me;
Listen to my evening prayer.

'MY ELDER SISTER WAS VERY BADLY HANDICAPPED with polio and she needed to be cared for all the time. I had to push her around in her bath chair. I was a terrible child, really. We lived in Chester and to get into the town we had to cross a big railway bridge. I used to push Gladys up, and when we got to the top, I let her go. Wasn't that an awful thing to do? Mind you, I ran very close to it so I could grab the handle and she was sort of steering herself. She never forgot it and to some extent I don't think the pour soul ever forgave me. She was frightened to death.

'My mother was the most remarkable woman. She used to sit up at night making dresses for the neighbours' children. One night she made five dresses! She was a very committed Christian and she taught us all to pray and seek forgiveness when we did anything wrong. This hymn was written deep in my heart because it was one that mother used to sing to us every night when she put us to bed. However difficult things were, however short of money she was, however much my father's debts would weigh on her, she always sang that to us at night, and I did the same with my children.'

Mary Whitehouse

JESUS, TENDER SHEPHERD, HEAR ME

ONWARD CHRISTIAN SOLDIERS

Onward, Christian soldiers
Marching as to war,
With the Cross of Jesus
Going on before.
Christ the royal Master
Leads against the foe
Forward into battle
See, his banners go.

(Refrain)
Onward, Christian soldiers
Marching as to war
With the Cross of Jesus
Going on before.

At the sign of triumph
Satan's host doth flee
On then, Christian soldiers
On to victory.
Hell's foundations quiver
At the shout of praise,
Brothers, lift your voices
Loud your anthems raise.

Like a mighty army
Moves the Church of God,
Brothers, we are treading
Where the saints have trod.
We are not divided
All one body we,
One in hope and doctrine
One in charity.

Crowns and thrones may perish,
Kingdoms rise and wane
But the Church of Jesus
Constant will remain.
Gates of hell can never
Gainst that Church prevail,
We have Christ's own promise
And that cannot fail.

Onward then ye people,
Join our happy throng,
Blend with ours your voices
In the triumph song.
Glory, laud and honour
Unto Christ the King,
This through countless ages
Men and angels sing.

'Every day I wake up in the morning with a hymn in my head. When I was seven I joined a church choir and I sang hymns. I loved them and I loved the theatricality of being a choir boy. After church service on a Sunday, we'd go to my grandmother's for bubble and squeak, and most of the family did bits and pieces. My sister would do a monologue or something. When it came to my turn, I was too shy to face them when I was singing, so I'd sit in the outside loo with the door open, and I'd be sitting there with my trousers round my ankles, surrounded by little squares of the *News of the World*, and I'd be singing *Onward Christian Soldiers* into the night! So that's one of the reasons why I've chosen it, but also I like the sound of it – it has a great lift to it.'

Sir Harry Secombe

ITV WEATHER PRESENTER SIAN LLOYD has stirring memories of her time at chapel in Neath, South Wales.

'I've chosen this hymn because I'm a chapel lass and on Whit Monday we would march, all the chapels of the area, behind our wonderful banner that we brought out once a year. We'd have our brand new clothes, little straw hats, patent shoes, and we'd march for the chapel and try and out-sing all the other chapels. We'd sing from the heart and *Onward Christian Soldiers* makes me think of that.'

Sian Lloyd

ABIDE WITH ME

'I DID A FEW CUP FINALS FOR TELEVISION and *Abide With Me* reduced me to tears every time. I would be rattling away with the commentary leading up to it but it is such a wonderful piece of music – so evocative, so emotional – that when the last notes drained away and in my earphones they said "Cue Moore", I actually had to take three or four deep breaths and a couple of gulps and give myself 15 or 20 seconds before I could go on. I could see all the people there who had sung it and I thought of my own children, because a hymn like that makes you think of so many things. So I couldn't possibly choose my favourite hymns without thinking of *Abide With Me* and all those wonderful Wembley moments.'

Brian Moore

'WHEN I WAS PLAYING AT LEICESTER CITY they only had a very limited number of Cup Final tickets – two for all the professionals. So we had to put our names in a hat and do a lucky dip, and one particular year I was the lucky one. Ten and six it cost and you stood – all open in those days. I'll never ever forget that first time they played *Abide With Me* just before the teams walked out. They actually gave you a sheet with the words on it and I'm not exaggerating, everybody sang it together. It was absolutely superb, it really was.'

Gordon Banks

'I FIND *ABIDE WITH ME* VERY MOVING AND VERY COMFORTING. I look for comfort in hymns. I was asked to sing it at the Cup Final but I turned it down because it's such a difficult thing to sing. I always get caught up in it when I'm singing it.'

Sir Harry Secombe

Abide with me, fast falls the eventide;
the darkness deepens; Lord, with me abide:
when other helpers fail, and comforts flee,
help of the helpless, O abide with me.

Swift to its close ebbs out life's little day;
earth's joys grow dim,
  its glories pass away;
change and decay in all around I see;
O thou who changest not, abide with me.

I need thy presence every passing hour;
what but thy grace can foil
  the tempter's power?
Who like thyself my guide and stay can be?
Through cloud and sunshine,
  Lord, abide with me.

I fear no foe with thee at hand to bless;
ills have no weight, and tears no bitterness.
Where is death's sting?
  Where, grave, thy victory?
I triumph still, if thou abide with me.

Hold thou thy cross before my closing eyes;
shine through the gloom,
  and point me to the skies;
heaven's morning breaks,
  and earth's vain shadows flee;
in life, in death,
O Lord, abide with me.

AMAZING GRACE

Amazing grace! How sweet the sound
that saved a wretch like me.
I once was lost, but now I'm found;
was blind but now I see.

Twas grace that taught my heart to fear,
and grace my fears relieved.
How precious did that grace appear
the hour I first believed.

Through many dangers, toils and snares
I have already come.
Tis grace hath brought me safe thus far,
and grace will lead me home.

The Lord has promised good to me,
his word my hope secures;
He will my shield and portion be
as long as life endures.

'MY MOTHER READ ME THE BIBLE SOMETIMES but my father was extremely right wing and admired the teachings of Hitler. This became a source of great friction between us, and there were dinner conversations where we were screaming at each other. That was a difficult side to the relationship which we gradually learnt to avoid.

'I think there has always been something unachieved throughout my life, the fact that I never managed to be the admired son that I would like to have been. My father didn't admire the fact that I was trying to be a painter, writer or musician.

'I once made an LP of 16 of my songs. It was produced by Des O'Connor who happened to hear me singing a song on television. The next morning he rang me up to ask if I'd written any other songs like that. *Amazing Grace* was very much in during the Sixties and was being sung by pop singers. So it links me to playing the guitar and a feeling of the culture that was coming out at that time.'

Lord Bath

'AMAZING GRACE IS SOMETHING that puts me in the right sort of mood to think, to consider. I lead a very busy life and it's very important to take time out to do these things. So I can think of nothing nicer than running a hot bath, with beautiful foaming bubble bath, beautiful perfumes, lighting a few candles, putting *Amazing Grace* on the CD player and just giving myself half-an-hour's relaxation and contemplating the world.'

Sian Lloyd

AMAZING GRACE

ALL CREATURES OF OUR GOD AND KING

All creatures of our God and King,
Lift up your voice and with us sing
Alleluia, alleluia!
Thou burning sun with golden beam,
Thou silver moon with softer gleam:

Oh praise him, O praise him,
Alleluia, alleluia, alleluia!

Thou rushing wind that art so strong,
Ye clouds that sail in heaven along,
O praise him, alleluia!
Thou rising morn, in praise rejoice,
Ye lights of evening, find a voice:

Thou flowing water, pure and clear,
Make music for thy Lord to hear,
Alleluia, alleluia!
Thou fire so masterful and bright,
That givest man both warmth and light:

Let all things their Creator bless,
And worship him in humbleness,
O praise him, alleluia!
Praise, praise the Father, praise the Son,
And praise the Spirit, Three in One.

'MY PARENTS WERE VERY POOR. My father was a labourer and mother was a barmaid, and we always ran out of money on Thursdays. We moved around a lot – I used to imagine that we did midnight flits because of the rent. But I didn't know that I was hard done by, because I lived in a basically poor area with poor people. It wasn't until I went to a kind of dancing charm school and then I came across the middle class that I realized that my background was pretty sparse.

'They loved my sister at dance school. She was an extremely good dancer and a very good singer. She was very pretty, but I don't think anybody thought anything of me there. They thought I was plain and talentless. Anyway, I knew after a year or two of dancing and ballet that I wanted to be an actress.

'The saddest thing in my life is that I didn't go to proper school. My last real schooling was when I was about 12. After that I was having two and a half hours of schooling a day, and that's absolutely inadequate. I know my parents did the best they could for me, and it was partly my choice too, but I feel deprived.

'The chapel I used to attend was very pretty and small and I loved the congregation – a wonderful mixture of farmers and all kinds of different people. This hymn is full of nature and puts me in mind of that lovely congregation.'

Jean Marsh

ALL HAIL THE POWER OF JESUS' NAME

All hail the power of Jesus' name
Let angels prostrate fall;
Bring forth the royal diadem
To crown him Lord of all.

Crown him, ye martyrs of your God,
Who from his altar call;
Praise him whose way of pain ye trod,
And crown him Lord of all.

Ye, prophets who our freedom won,
Ye searchers, great and small,
By whom the work of truth is done,
Now crown him Lord of all.

Let every tribe and every tongue
To him their hearts enthral:
Lift high the universal song,
And crown him Lord of all.

'I CAN REMEMBER MY LAST YEAR AT SCHOOL, delivering milk, during the summer vacation for the Brightside and Carbrook Co-op, and going to houses where, in those days, the 1950s, a woman couldn't afford to buy a bottle of milk on Fridays because she had no money until her husband came home with the wages in the evening. And I can remember the trick we used to play. The milkman used to decide whether she was worth a bit of help. If he saw her smoking he thought she wasn't worth help, she was squandering her money. If she looked like the deserving poor he would carefully take the lid off the bottle, pour the milk into her jug, put the tin foil lid back on, smash the bottle, and record it as a break, giving her a free bottle of milk. And I can remember thinking a decent society wouldn't have people who can't afford a bottle of milk on a Friday, and a decent society wouldn't expect milkmen to make decisions between the deserving and undeserving poor. For me, that was the ideological drive towards socialism.

'I chose this hymn because it is a good rousing hymn which enlightens the process of belief and I think gives hymn-singing a good name.'

Lord Roy Hattersley

ALL PEOPLE THAT ON EARTH DO DWELL

All people that on earth do dwell,
sing to the Lord with cheerful voice;
him serve with fear, his praise forth tell,
come ye before him and rejoice.

The Lord, ye know, is God indeed,
without our aid he did us make;
we are his folk, he doth us feed,
and for his sheep he doth us take.

O enter then his gates with praise,
approach with joy his courts unto;
praise, laud and bless his name always,
for it is seemly so to do.

For why? the Lord our God is good:
his mercy is for ever sure;
his truth at all times firmly stood,
and shall from age to age endure.

To Father, Son and Holy Ghost,
the God whom heaven and earth adore,
from men and from the angel-host
be praise and glory evermore.

ALL PEOPLE THAT ON EARTH DO DWELL

'I WAS BROUGHT UP ON A COUNCIL ESTATE IN DAGENHAM. It was particularly tough during the war. I remember one bitter occasion when there was a problem the first time we were evacuated to Wiltshire. My mother didn't get on with the lady who looked after us so we came back unexpectedly, but we didn't have any money. We got as far as a London station and my mother was almost paralyzed. She didn't know what to do. I can remember the fear we all had and then suddenly a neighbour was spotted and took us home.

'Seeing people killed in the war affected my faith because, as a young boy growing up in that kind of situation, it made me wonder if in fact there is a God. And if there is a God, is he knowable? And if he is knowable, does he really care for us? I asked a lot of questions of that nature. Then, when I was about 16, I went along to a church youth club (I have to say, rather sceptically – I didn't regard myself as particularly religious) and got caught up in the youth activity. I remember enjoying it enormously and being made to think more seriously about life. I started on a Christian journey – and that journey continues to this very day, because I think doubt is a very important part of faith itself. I still continue to question the love of God, but my faith has become stronger and deeper as the years have gone by. And I remember at the age of 17, crossing a line. I would call it a conversion experience of crossing the line from questioning to acceptance: that God actually loves me, and loves everybody, and that God is knowable, and his name is Jesus. That was deeply precious and important.

'When we were evacuated to Bradford-on-Avon during the war, our family were adopted by Christ Church in the town. Thank God for them. I can remember going along to the village school and to the church and this hymn was sung. It's my earliest memory of a hymn and it reminds me of the security and love of God.'

Dr George Carey, Archbishop of Canterbury

ALL THINGS BRIGHT AND BEAUTIFUL

'YOU'VE GOT TO GIVE RATHER THAN TAKE ALL THE TIME, and you've got to believe that you are helped if you say a prayer by God himself. That's why I like *All Things Bright and Beautiful*.

'Women have more to give than men. Our job as women is to make people happy. Happiness is a thing which is difficult to find. A great many people are very unhappy in the world.

'Diana tried to help people and did help people in a great way, and therefore we ought to be very grateful that we've had her. She was looking for love, she was looking for something different in her life to what she had, and that was the tragedy that killed her. What she adored was children. She was so fond of them and always wanted children to be happy, especially those who were brought up badly.'

Dame Barbara Cartland

'THE ORGANIZATION CHILD LINE stands for the adult world holding out their hands to suffering children, saying we care about you. We must remember the message that our children are precious. We must look after them. This is a children's hymn and the sound of children singing this hymn is just delightful. I sang it myself when I was four or five years old, so I probably know all the words. Also, if there is a God, and I hope there is a God, it says something to me about the beauty of the world he created.'

Esther Rantzen

All things bright and beautiful,
All creatures great and small,
All things wise and wonderful,
The Lord God made them all.

Each little flower that opens,
Each little bird that sings,
He made their glowing colours,
He made their tiny wings:

The purple-headed mountain,
The river running by,
The sunset and the morning,
That brightens up the sky:

The cold wind in the winter,
The pleasant summer sun,
The ripe fruits in the garden,
He made them every one:

The tall trees in the greenwood,
the meadows for our play,
the rushes by the water,
to gather ev'ry day.

He gave us eyes to see them,
And lips that we might tell
How great is God Almighty,
Who has made all things well.

BE THOU MY VISION

Be thou my vision, O Lord of my heart,
naught be all else to me save that thou art;
thou my best thought in the day
  and the night,
waking or sleeping, thy presence my light.

Be thou my wisdom, be thou my true word,
I ever with thee and thou with me, Lord;
thou my great Father, and I thy true heir;
thou in me dwelling, and I in thy care.

Be thou my breast-plate, my sword
  for the fight,
be thou my armour, and be thou my might,
thou my soul's shelter, and thou
  my high tower,
raise thou me heavenward,
  O Power of my power.

Riches I need not, nor all the
  world's praise,
thou mine inheritance through all my days;
thou, and thou only, the first in my heart,
high King of heaven, my treasure thou art!

High King of heaven when battle is done,
grant heaven's joy to me,
  O bright heav'ns sun;
Christ of my own heart, whatever befall,
still be my vision, O Ruler of all.

'I BECAME A COMMITTED CHRISTIAN IN 1986. At the same time I discovered that low fat eating would help my gallstone problem. Eating less fat changed my figure and asking God into my heart changed my life.

'Following extensive trials of my low fat diet, I wrote *The Hip & Thigh Diet*, which was fantastically successful. My career changed dramatically from the moment God came into my life.

'I think the words '*Be thou my vision*' are so true. The hymn makes you realize that we are only what we are because of how God loves us, and we should never forget that.'

Rosemary Conley

BE THOU MY VISION

COUNT YOUR BLESSINGS

When upon life's billows you are
  tempest tossed,
When you are discouraged, thinking all is lost,
Count your many blessings,
  name them one by one,
And it will surprise you
  what the Lord hath done.

Count your blessings, name them one by one,
Count your blessings,
  see what God hath done;
Count your blessings, name them one by one,
And it will surprise you
  what the Lord hath done.

Are you ever burdened with a load of care?
Does the cross seem heavy
  you are called to bear?

Count your many blessings,
  every doubt will fly,
And you will be singing as the days go by.

When you look at others
  with their lands and gold,
Think that Christ has promised you
  His wealth untold.
Count your many blessings,
  money cannot buy
Your reward in heaven,
  nor your home on high.

So amid the conflict,
  whether great or small,
Do not be discouraged, God is over all,
Count your many blessings,
  angels will attend,
Help and comfort give you
  to your journey's end.

ERIC SYKES BELIEVES IN MAKING THE MOST OF LIFE. 'I still do stage work and it's quite easy really. I learn the parts not from reading the script, which I cannot do nowadays, but instead they record it for me on a cassette. As far as the stage itself goes, I have somebody to take me to the door through which I make my entrance and, once you get on it, it's so well lit you can't really miss it. As soon as it starts to get dark, I know I'm near the pit so I back off.

'My hearing is done through my glasses – they're "listening" glasses. I've had these for 25 years, but for the 25 years I didn't have them, I couldn't hear a laugh. I used to go through my act, and not a laugh from the audience. Then I got these and I realized I hadn't been getting any!

'I look upon the plus side: my glass is half full rather than half empty. And that's why I like *Count Your Blessings*.'

COUNT YOUR BLESSINGS

DEAR LORD AND FATHER OF MANKIND

Dear Lord and Father of mankind,
Forgive our foolish ways!
Re-clothe us in our rightful mind,
In purer lives thy service find,
In deeper reverence praise.

In simple trust like theirs who heard,
Beside the Syrian sea,
The gracious calling of the Lord,
Let us, like them, without a word
Rise up and follow thee.

O Sabbath rest by Galilee!
O calm of hills above,
Where Jesus knelt to share with thee,
The silence of eternity,
Interpreted by love!

Drop thy still dews of quietness,
Till all our strivings cease;
Take from our souls the strain and stress,
And let our ordered lives confess
The beauty of thy peace.

Breathe through the heats of our desire
Thy coolness and thy balm;
Let sense be dumb let flesh retire;
Speak through the earthquake,
  wind, and fire,
O still small voice of calm!

SUE JOHNSTON (BARBARA FROM *THE ROYLE FAMILY*) explains how pursuing an acting career put her on a collision course with her father.
'He didn't like it; he didn't like it at all. My dad was very sad that I didn't go to university. He missed out on that himself, and when I went to grammar school he was very proud and he really wanted me to go to university. So when I was determined to go into acting, we did come into very heavy conflict about it. I hated hurting him, I couldn't bear it. He only had to put a certain expression on his face and I'd crumble. The only other time we really fell out was when I dyed my hair. I always had very dark hair and the first time I dyed it platinum blonde, he locked the door as he saw me coming up the path and wouldn't open it till I went back to the hairdressers to have it changed back!

'*Dear Lord and Father of Mankind* was one of the choices at my first wedding. I just think the words and melody are beautiful, and it's always meant an awful lot to me.'

Sue Johnston

FAITH OF OUR FATHERS

Faith of our fathers, living still in
spite of dungeon, fire and sword;
O, how our hearts beat high with
Joy whene'er we hear that
Glorious word!

Faith of our fathers! Holy Faith!
We will be true to thee till death,
We will be true to thee till death.

Our fathers, chained in prisons dark,
Were still in heart and conscience free;
How sweet would be their children's fate,
If they, like them, could die for thee!

Faith of our fathers, Mary's prayers
Shall win our country back to thee;
And through the truth that comes
  from God
England shall then indeed be free.

Faith of our fathers, we will love
Both friend and foe in all our strife,
And preach thee too, as love knows how,
By kindly words and virtuous life.

'*FAITH OF OUR FATHERS* TAKES ME BACK to my days as a young boy aged seven to twelve or thirteen. My father, mother, brother, sister and I would sit around the fire learning sonnets and singing hymns. I can remember that I could harmonise any song that we would sing – it's a part of my life I cherish lovingly. Sadly, this kind of family life seems gone forever.

Faith of our fathers is a hymn that we in Ireland learn from the cradle days, it was the one song I learnt, as I thought it remarkable to sing in a foreign language!

Although, secretly, I always would have loved to have been a successful musician, alas, 'Old Father Time' has beaten me to the piano.'

Frank Carson

FAITH OF OUR FATHERS

HE WHO WOULD VALIANT BE

He who would valiant be
Gainst all disaster,
Let him in constancy
Follow the master.
There's no discouragement
Shall make him once relent
His first avowed intent
to be a pilgrim.

Who so beset him round
with dismal stories,
Do but themselves confound
His strength the more is.

No foes shall stay his might,
Though he with giants fight:
He will make good his right
to be a pilgrim.

Since, Lord, thou dost defend
Us with thy Spirit,
We know we at the end
Shall life inherit.
Then fancies flee away!
I'll fear not what men say,
I'll labour night and day
To be a pilgrim.

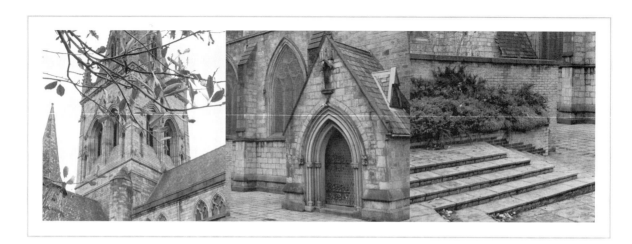

'I WAS SPEAKING AT ONE OF OUR MAIN UNIVERSITIES and the hall was absolutely full, about 2,000 people. I noticed there were three rows across the front and the young fellows there were sitting very straight and very grim, no smiles or anything like that. I thought, hello, that's where we're going to get a bit of trouble. Well, they all rose and one of them had got a tin of blue paint and he threw this tin of paint straight at me. It hit me in the tummy, ran all the way down my clothes, but I didn't stop. When I finished, I walked off the platform and one of the students was standing there crying. He said: "Mary, I am so sorry. Will you forgive me?" I just put my arms around him and gave him a big hug and said: "Yes, of course."

'I often met opposition of some kind, and I used to say the words of *He Who Would Valiant Be* before I started. That gave me backbone. I was really ready for the blue tin. I mean, I didn't know it was coming, but I was ready for anything really.'

Mary Whitehouse

'THERE WERE A FEW MOMENTS THAT YOU SAVOURED as a child in Sunday School and in the church itself, and one was when this hymn came up. Not only was it one that almost everybody knew, so for once the entire congregation sang at a volume that was slightly above that of the organ, but also you could change the words. And for all of us in Sunday School, it was *He Who Would Valiant Be*… to be a pilchard!'

Rick Wakeman

'THE MUSIC IS STIRRING, THE WORDS ARE VERY IMPORTANT and I think whatever your background, *He Who Would Valiant Be* is inspirational. I can remember belting it out like a good 'un in school assembly with my friends.'

Esther Rantzen

SOUL OF MY SAVIOUR

FRANK MCCOURT RECALLS HOW HE SAVED UP £50 and set off for a new life in America at the age of 19.

'My education ended at the age of 13 and I had no skills, no self-esteem. I didn't know my way around the world and I had to learn to be civilized. I didn't know clothes, I didn't know food, I didn't know drink, I didn't know one vegetable from another. I knew the potato – you couldn't fool me on the potato – or turnips, or peas. That was the extent of my vegetable education. But I was a voracious reader and in New York I fell into a menial job in a hotel, cleaning the lobby, and two blocks away from that hotel was the 46th Street library. It's a magnificent place, an oasis in the heart of New York, the one place that hasn't changed. It was a refuge for me, but then I was drafted into the army and sent to Germany. I spent two years as a dog trainer in the canine corps and they sent me to clerk's school where I learned to type. When I got out of the army they had the GI Bill which was a gorgeous piece of legislation that enabled people who'd served their time in the army to go to school. But I talked my way into New York University. I jumped over the whole high school and secondary school thing. They let me into university and after four years I graduated and became a teacher. As soon as I opened my mouth, the students wanted to know all about Ireland. They were fascinated.

'Nowadays I feel like a New Yorker. I like the virility and vitality of the streets there. I stand at street corners, looking for little moments of drama when the light turns red. Then one car bumps another and the two drivers, who are from completely different parts of the world, say nasty things about each other's mothers. And they're opening the door to get out when the light turns green. Then they're gone, but you've had 20 seconds of pure Greek drama which could have ended tragically. That's what I like about New York – there's always something going on in the streets.

'*Soul of my Saviour* takes me back to Limerick. We had benediction in a huge church and this is the one hymn that echoes in me. It was one of those celebration songs and it used to reverberate around the whole place, and it would give me a happy feeling.'

Frank McCourt

Soul of my Saviour,
Sanctify my breast;
Body of Christ,
Be thou my saving guest;
Blood of my Saviour,
Bathe me in thy tide,
Wash me with water
Flowing from thy side.

Strength and protection
May thy Passion be;
O blessed Jesus,
Hear and answer me;
Deep in thy wounds, Lord,
Hide and shelter me;
Shall I never,
Never part from thee.

WHO WOULD TRUE VALOUR SEE

Who would true valour see,
let him come hither.
one here will constant be,
come wind, come weather,
there's no discouragement
shall make him once relent
his first avowed intent
to be a pilgrim.

Whoso beset him round
with dismal stories
do but themselves confound
his strength the more is.

No lion can him fright
he'll live with a giant fight
but he will have the right
to be a pilgrim.

No goblin nor foul friend
can daunt his spirit,
he knows he at the end
shall life inherit.
Then, fancies fly away
he'll no fear what men say
he'll labour night and day
to be a pilgrim.

'I BECAME PREGNANT WHEN I WAS STILL QUITE YOUNG, after university. Life was easier then for an unmarried mother than it is today when they are seen as some sort of burden on the state. Nowadays they have no choice – the pressure to keep the baby is very great whereas the pressure used to be to have the baby adopted. I think children now who were adopted see it as the mother's failure somehow to love. It wasn't like that. If you loved your child but couldn't support it, you would give it up for adoption because there was no social security, no housing. I thought I could manage, so I kept my child. People were very supportive, extremely helpful. It was inconvenient and difficult, but I didn't go along bowing my head in shame.

'*Who Would True Valour See* is a stirring hymn and one always wanted to be that person, the one who was going to be valiant in the face of goblin and foul fiend. You would take notes of these and you would fight your way through to the end. And I just thought that was wonderful.'

Fay Weldon

JERUSALEM

And did those feet in ancient time
walk upon England's mountains green?
And was the holy lamb of God
on England's pleasant pastures seen?
And did the countenance divine
shine forth upon our clouded hills?
And was Jerusalem builded here
among those dark satanic mills?

Bring me my bow of burning gold!
Bring me my arrows of desire!
Bring me my spear O clouds unfold!
Bring my my chariot of fire!
I will not cease from mental fight,
nor shall my sword sleep in my hand
till we have built Jerusalem
in England's green and pleasant land.

JERUSALEM

'**M**Y MOTHER WAS THE HEAD of a religious nomination and her influence was a very profound one. I was brought up on the Bible and I had a conflict on the first day with my Bible teacher, Miss Babcock. She said God was angry and I said – I was about five at the time – "No, Miss Babcock, God is love." So I was removed from the class and forced to sit in another room while she taught. And she complained to my mother!

'I was taught as a child that there was a conflict in the Old Testament between the Kings who exercised power and the Prophets who preached righteousness. I was brought up on the Prophets and not the Kings, and it is a very simple principle which I find helps me in modern politics. It is people who've got something to say that I want to listen to, not necessarily the people who've got to the top of the greasy pole and are now bossing everybody else about.

'*Jerusalem* relates the idea of the heavenly city to the daily life. Those dark satanic mills, the terrible conditions of industrial England, but give me my arrows of desire and we will build Jerusalem in England's green and pleasant land: that's very much the social message. It's a hymn that people love and appreciate, and it has some meaning politically as well as being about the Holy City itself.'

Tony Benn

'LISTENING TO HYMNS, I ALWAYS HAD A
SENSE THAT THERE WAS A GUARDIAN
ANGEL, SOMEBODY WATCHING OVER ME.'

JEAN MARSH

'MY MOTHER WAS A REMARKABLE
WOMAN... HOWEVER DIFFICULT
THINGS WERE, HOWEVER SHORT
OF MONEY SHE WAS, HOWEVER
MUCH MY FATHER'S DEBTS WOULD
WEIGH ON HER, SHE ALWAYS SANG
THAT TO US AT NIGHT, AND I DID
THE SAME WITH MY CHILDREN.'

MARY WHITEHOUSE

MY FAVOURITE HYMNS

'EVERY DAY I WAKE UP IN THE MORNING WITH A HYMN IN MY HEAD.'

SIR HARRY SECOMBE

'I DID A FEW CUP
FINALS FOR TELEVISION
AND ABIDE WITH ME
REDUCED ME TO TEARS
EVERY TIME.'

BRIAN MOORE

'AMAZING GRACE IS SOMETHING THAT
PUTS ME IN THE RIGHT SORT OF MOOD
TO THINK, TO CONSIDER.'

SIAN LLOYD

'IT'S MY EARLIEST MEMORY OF A HYMN
AND IT REMINDS ME OF THE SECURITY
AND LOVE OF GOD.'

GEORGE CAREY

'SOUL OF MY SAVIOUR TAKES ME BACK TO LIMERICK. WE HAD BENEDICTION IN A HUGE CHURCH AND THIS IS ONE HYMN THAT ECHOES IN ME. IT WAS ONE OF THOSE CELEBRATION SONGS AND IT USED TO REVERBERATE AROUND THE WHOLE PLACE, AND IT WOULD GIVE ME A HAPPY FEELING.'

FRANK McCOURT

'AVE MARIA IS VERY BEAUTIFUL. MY LATE WIFE, PADDY, WAS A SOPRANO AND SHE USED TO SING IT IN CHURCH. GOD, IT WAS BEAUTIFUL.'

SPIKE MILLIGAN

'I LOOK UPON THE PLUS SIDE: MY GLASS IS
HALF FULL RATHER THAN HALF EMPTY. AND
THAT'S WHY I LIKE COUNT YOUR BLESSINGS.'

ERIC SYKES

'DEAR LORD AND FATHER OF MANKIND WAS ONE OF THE CHOICES AT MY FIRST WEDDING. I JUST THINK THE WORDS AND MELODY ARE BEAUTIFUL.'

SUE JOHNSTON

MY FAVOURITE HYMNS

'I CHOSE HAIL QUEEN OF HEAVEN BECAUSE THE MOTHER IN ANY FAMILY IS PROBABLY THE MOST IMPORTANT PERSON.'

FRANK CARSON

'HYMNS WERE MY FIRST RELATIONSHIP WITH
MUSIC AND IMMORTAL, INVISIBLE IS JUST A GOOD
RIP-ROARING ANTHEM.'

TOYAH WILCOX

MY FAVOURITE HYMNS

'YOU'VE GOT TO GIVE RATHER THAN TAKE ALL THE TIME,
AND YOU'VE GOT TO BELIEVE THAT YOU ARE HELPED, IF
YOU SAY A PRAYER, BY GOD HIMSELF. THAT'S WHY I LIKE
ALL THINGS BRIGHT AND BEAUTIFUL.'

DAME BARBARA CARTLAND

'YOU CAN'T LEAVE
CHURCH HAVING
HEARD PRAISE TO
THE LORD, THE
ALMIGHTY THE KING
OF CREATION
WITHOUT FEELING
PRETTY GOOD ABOUT
THE WORLD AND
MAYBE EVEN NOT TOO
BAD ABOUT YOURSELF.'

BRIAN MOORE

'I DON'T SEE GOD AS IN A SENSE AN ENTITY,
I SEE GOD AS AN ALL-PERVADING GOODNESS.'

DENISE ROBERTSON

'WHO WOULD TRUE VALOUR SEE IS A STIRRING HYMN AND ONE ALWAYS WANTED TO BE THAT PERSON, THE ONE WHO WAS GOING TO BE VALIANT.'

FAY WELDON

MY FAVOURITE HYMNS

LOVE DIVINE ALL LOVES EXCELLING

'THIS IS MY FAVOURITE HYMN. Michelle (Dotrice) and I chose it for our wedding. We were married in a house we'd rented in the Catskill Mountains in New York. I was doing *The Equalizer* and we were married by the local judge. When we first met him, Michelle and I looked at each other and we were appalled. We both went white as a sheet because he looked about 12 years old! I said: "Have you ever married anybody before?" And he said: "You'll be my second." I thought, wow, he's done it once before, that's all right, and we had this beautiful ceremony. Karen, Michelle's sister, had a little tape recorder and put on a cassette of the hymns. And we all sang. So *Love Divine* has wonderful, wonderful connotations, wonderful memories.'

Edward Woodward

'BETTY AND I HAD A VERY UNPROMISING START to our marriage because on our wedding day there was a snow storm. Now that's a pretty icy omen. Then we got to the reception and the cake collapsed – another icy omen. But we have been happy for 46 years, so the omens weren't all that accurate. *Love Divine* was one of the hymns we had at our wedding. We went to Paignton for a week's honeymoon and on Torquay station I jumped out of the train to get the local evening football paper. She has never allowed me to forget that!'

Brian Moore

Love divine, all loves excelling,
joy of heav'n, to earth come down,
fix in us thy humble dwelling,
all thy faithful mercies crown.

Jesu, thou art all compassion,
pure, unbounded love thou art;
visit us with thy salvation,
enter ev'ry trembling heart.

Come, almighty to deliver,
let us all thy life receive;
suddenly return, and never,
never more thy temples leave.

Thee we would be always blessing,
serve thee as thy hosts above,
pray, and praise thee, without ceasing,
glory in thy perfect love.

Finish then thy new creation,
pure and sinless let us be;
let us see thy great salvation,
perfectly restored in thee.

Changed from glory into glory,
till in heav'n we take our place,
till we cast our crowns before thee,
lost in wonder love and praise!

LOVE DIVINE ALL LOVES EXCELLING

FIGHT THE GOOD FIGHT

Fight the good fight with all thy might,
Christ is thy strength, and Christ
    thy right;
Lay hold on life, and it shall be
Thy joy and crown eternally.

Run the straight race through God's
    good grace,
Life up thine eyes, and seek his face;
Life with its way before us lies,
Christ is the path, and Christ the prize.

Cast care aside, upon thy Guide
Lean, and his mercy will provide;
Lean, and thy trusting soul shall prove
Christ is its life, and Christ its love.

Faint not nor fear, his arms are near,
He changeth not, and thou art dear;
Only believe, and thou shalt see
That Christ is all in all to thee.

'I LIKE THE FUN AND VIGOUR OF HYMNS AND THE CAMARADERIE, almost, in a church, of people singing together. When I was at boarding school in Somerset, we had morning chapel every single morning and two services on Sunday and, because I sang in the choir, we also had choir practices. I liked the theatre of it. I enjoyed the break from routine. For me it was like sport – the chapel was something that kept one out of the classroom.

'I pray when I'm in trouble, so I pray quite often! I pray when things aren't going well. I'm like those people on an aeroplane when it shudders, I then look up and expect there to be a God. I think in the end I do believe there has to be a superior being, only because the most beautiful things on earth are not man made.

'I suppose by nature I'm an enthusiast – there's not a cynical bone in my body. I like to achieve, I like to do things, I don't have time for cynics. In fact, I'd rather be a naïve enthusiast than a cynic. *Fight The Good Fight* is a hymn where you can stand up, join in and have a good go. It's us against the cynics.'

Lord Jeffrey Archer

GLORIOUS THINGS OF THEE ARE SPOKEN

Glorious things of thee are spoken,
Zion, city of our God!
He whose word cannot be broken
Formed thee for his own abode:
On the Rock of Ages founded,
What can shake thy sure repose?
With salvation's walls surrounded,
Thou may'st smile at all thy foes.

See, the streams of living waters,
Springing from eternal love,
Well supply thy sons and daughters,
And all fear of want remove.
Who can faint while such a river
Ever flows their thirst to assuage?
Grace which, like the Lord, the giver,
Never fails from age to age.

Saviour, if of Zion's city
I, through grace, a member am,
Let the world deride or pity,
I will glory in thy name:
Fading is the worldling's pleasure,
All his boasted pomp and show;
Solid joys and lasting treasure
None but Zion's children know.

'THIS IS A VERY ENCOURAGING HYMN. I THINK IT MAKES one feel more energetic, more lively if you like, almost more spiritual.

'I'm fortunate that I have had a wonderful wife – Elizabeth – standing by me. When I've been attacked, she stood by me. She stood by me when I was breaking down in health in the war, and she stood by me when I've been attacked over Myra Hindley. So that's all that matters really for me – her opinion. But *Glorious Things Of Thee Are Spoken* sometimes gives me extra strength.'

Lord Frank Pakenham Longford

GO DOWN MOSES

When Israel was in Egypt's land,
  Let my people go.
Oppressed so hard they could not stand,
  Let my people go.

Go down Moses
Way Down in Egypt's land
Tell old Pharoah to let my people go.

Thus saith the Lord bold Moses said,
  Let my people go.
If not I'll smite your first-born dead,
  Let my people go.

Go down Moses
Way down in Egypt's land
Tell old Pharoah to let my people go.

BLACK WRITER AND POET DR MAYA ANGELOU WAS RAISED amid the racial bigotry of America's Deep South in the 1930s.

'I remember being in a cocoon of love but surrounded by hate – racism, segregation, the Ku Klux Klan. My grandmother took us to church on Sunday, all day. In the late afternoon we'd go home and then Monday night was a poem meeting, Tuesday night was prayer meeting, Wednesday night was choir practice, the only day we didn't go to church was Saturday. We used Saturday to prepare to go to church all day Sunday.

'I love hymns, I count on them. If things are going very badly for me I sing; if things are going very well for me I sing, always starting with hymns.

'I chose *Go Down Moses* because it speaks of hope. The African American used the Jews, Israel and Egypt as metaphors for slavery, for cruelty. That God could say to Moses, "Go and tell Pharaoh to let my people go," was just remarkable, so full of hope.'

Dr Maya Angelou

GO DOWN MOSES

GRACIOUS SPIRIT, HOLY GHOST

Gracious spirit, Holy ghost,
Taught by thee, we covet most
Of thy gifts at Pentecost,
Holy, heavenly love.

Love is kind, and suffers long,
Love is meek, and thinks no wrong,
Love than death itself more strong;
Therefore give us love.

From the overshadowing
Of thy gold and silver wing
Shed on us, who to thee sing,
Holy, heavenly love.

'I KNOW GHOSTS EXIST BECAUSE I'VE SEEN ONE. I had an experience when I was young, at the old house in Derbyshire in which I was born and where my doctor father had a surgery. Attached to it was a cottage and our bathroom was on the top floor of this cottage. One day I was sitting on the loo – which is probably a good place to be when you see a ghost – and in the doorway was a grey shape with eyes. I felt absolutely petrified, but after a while it just went.

'I had another experience when my daughter Edwina died. She was 18 months old, and the grief my wife Sarah and myself went through was just unbelievable. The grief was physically painful and I didn't know how I was going to get through her funeral. We hadn't eaten, we'd lived on hot chocolate, that was all we could manage. Then on the morning of the funeral – four days after her death – I woke up and I saw the face of Edwina smiling, glowing in gold. I saw her, there's no doubt about that, and I felt a colossal weight lifted from me and Sarah. It was a such a feeling of comfort and relief. In my view, the Church lets people down in moments of grief. Life does go on and it goes on in a very positive way.

'*Gracious Spirit, Holy Ghost* is attributed to Paul, who we believe from some of the readings was a mystic. He would understand about the spiritual content, the ability to be a seer or a prophet, which the truly spiritual people are. He talks about mysteries. But of course at the end he says the greatest of all is love, which it is. Love really is the essence of everything.'

William Roache

GRACIOUS SPIRIT, HOLY GHOST

HAIL QUEEN OF HEAVEN

Hail Queen of heaven, the ocean star,
Guide of the wand'rer here below;
Thrown on life's surge, we claim thy care;
save us from peril and from woe.
Mother of Christ, star of the sea,
Pray for the wand'rer, pray for me.

O gentle, chaste and spotless maid
We sinners make our prayers through thee;
Remind thy Son that he has paid
The price of our iniquity.
Virgin most pure, star of the sea,
Pray for the sinner, pray for me.

Sojourners in this vale of tears,
To thee, blest advocate, we cry;
Pity our sorrows, calm our fears,
And soothe with hope our misery.
Refuge in grief, star of the sea,
Pray for the mourner, pray for me.

And while to him who reigns above,
In Godhead One, in persons Three,
The source of life, of grace, of love,
Homage we pay on bended knee,
Do thou, bright Queen, star of the sea,
Pray for thy children, pray for me.

HAIL QUEEN OF HEAVEN

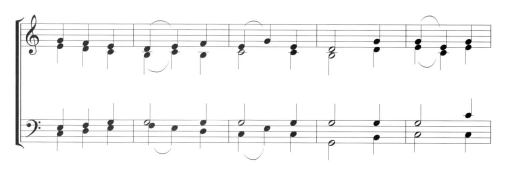

'THE QUEEN IS A LOVELY PERSON. I was doing a Royal Variety Performance but at the end of my spot, instead of bowing then walking off, I thought I'd stop. I had a gag in my head. I looked up at the Royal Box and said: "By the way, Your Majesty, I'm at the Open University doing biology and engineering, so let me know if you ever want your corgis welded." Well, of course, the place went into an uproar. Des O'Connor aged 40 years! And everybody looked at the Royal Box and the Queen was laughing her head off. Afterwards, she came down to me and said: "Frank, that was a very funny joke about the corgis. Can I use it?" I said: "Only, Your Majesty, if I can use it on my CV that you're stealing my material!"

'I chose *Hail Queen of Heaven* because the mother in any family is probably the most important person. When the mother goes, all the ties seem to go. When I go, they'll probably all laugh their heads off, but when mammy goes that will be the biggest break of all.'

Frank Carson

SWING LOW SWEET CHARIOT

'IN ALMOST ALL AFRICAN AMERICAN MUSIC there is a longing for home because we were wrenched so cruelly from the homeland. So in this song, "comin' for to carry me home" represents the yearning for an actual home where one is not the object of hate and revilement and ignorance.

'When I went to Africa I was blown away by the modes of dress and the ways of cooking food. I was startled to find out that many of the things with which I had grown up actually had African origins. It was amazing to see people who looked like my uncle, my cousin, my brother and to realize that, whereas in the United States, black people are a tenth of the population, here I was in a country where everybody was black. It was heady.'

Dr Maya Angelou

Swing low, sweet chariot,
Comin' for to carry me home.
Swing low, sweet chariot,
Comin' for to carry me home.

I looked over Jordan and what did I see?
Comin' for to carry me home?
A band of angels comin' after me,
Comin for to carry me home.

Swing low, sweet chariot,
Comin' for to carry me home.
Swing low, sweet chariot,
Comin' for to carry me home.

If you get there before I do,
Comin' for to carry me home,
Tell all my friends I'm comin' too,
Comin' for to carry me home.

Swing low, sweet chariot,
Comin' for to carry me home.
Swing low, sweet chariot,
Comin' for to carry me home.

SWING LOW SWEET CHARIOT

HOW SWEET THE NAME
OF JESUS SOUNDS

How sweet the name of Jesus sounds
in a believer's ear
It soothes his sorrows, heals his wounds
and drives away his fear.

It makes the wounded spirit whole,
and calms the troubled breast;
'tis manna to the hungry soul,
and to the weary rest.

Dear name! the rock on which I build,
my shield and hiding place,
my never failing treasury filled
with boundless stores of grace.

Jesus! my Shepherd, Brother, Friend
my Prophet, Priest and King,
my Lord, my Life, my Way, my End,
accept the praise I bring.

Weak is the effort of my heart,
and cold my warmest thought;
but when I see thee as thou art,
I'll praise thee as I ought.

Till then I would thy love proclaim
with every fleeting breath;
and may the music of thy name
refresh my soul in death.

'MY MOTHER WAS QUITE KEEN ON ME BECOMING A VICAR and I was persuaded to read the lesson one week. I was so nervous I did it like Sandy Powell. Everybody started laughing but the vicar didn't like it at all, so that was me finished. I was very relieved really.

'But she was lovely, my mother. She was one of those people that when anything went wrong, the neighbours called for her. She was like an unofficial district nurse. This was her favourite hymn and I find it very comforting myself. The words are so good. Soothing his sorrows, healing his wounds, driving away his fear – there's something very comforting about that when you're not feeling too well or you get a bit brassed off with things.'

Sir Harry Secombe

IMMORTAL, INVISIBLE GOD ONLY WISE

Immortal invisible, God only wise
in light inaccessible hid from our eyes
most blèssed, most glorious,
   the Ancient of Days
almighty, victorious,
   thy great name we praise.

Unresting, unhasting,
and silent as light
nor wanting, nor wasting,
   thou rulest in might
thy justice like mountains
   high soaring above
thy clouds which are fountains
   of goodness and love.

To all life thou givest,
   to both great and small
in all life thou livest,
   the true life of all;
we blossom and flourish
   as leaves on the tree
and wither and perish;
   but naught changeth thee.

Great Father of glory,
   pure Father of light
thine angels adore thee,
   all veiling their sight
all laud we would render
   O help us to see
'tis only the splendour
   of light hideth thee.

'I WAS BORN WITH A TWISTED SPINE and I had one leg longer than the other. I had to do physio twice a day to learn to hold my spine straight because if I didn't learn to do it, the only other way was a body cast, which I didn't want. I suppose I was bullied at school for the first ten years but then I was such a fighter, the tables turned quite radically. I was probably bullied more for the lisp and the speech impediment, because I had to have vocabulary lessons to learn to speak properly. I couldn't form words at all. But by the time I was 11, I was so determined and so strong that nothing was going to get in my way.

'I've always felt that if I'm going to be remembered for anything it's for women surging forward to make their place on earth, not to be secondary creatures. Hymns were my first relationship with music and *Immortal, Invisible* is just a good rip-roaring anthem. There's something about me like that image of Boadicea on the chariot, going forward into the future ready for battle and not letting anything get in your way. This hymn fits that image.'

Toyah Wilcox

JESU, LOVER OF MY SOUL

Jesu, lover of my soul,
Let me to thy bosom fly,
While the nearer waters roll,
While the tempest still is high:
Hide me, O my Saviour, hide,
Till the storm of life is past;
Safe into the haven guide,
O receive my soul at last.

Other refuge have I none,
Hangs my helpless soul on thee;
Leave ah! leave me not alone,
Still support and comfort me.

All my trust on thee is stayed,
All my help from thee I bring;
Cover my defenceless head
With the shadow of thy wing.

Plenteous grace with thee is found,
Grace to cover all my sin
Let the healing streams abound,
Make and keep me pure within,
Thou of life the fountain art,
Freely let me take of thee,
Spring thou up within my heart,
Rise to all eternity.

'MY FATHER WAS A BAPTIST LAY PREACHER, so was my grandfather. My father said the worst thing you can do is force a kid to go to church, because then the first thing he'll want to do when he's old enough is leave it. So you only go if you want to go. I loved it. Church was fantastic at first because it solidified the things I believed in. It went wrong in later years, because I reached the age of 18 and I enjoyed a drink or ten, and I smoked like a chimney, and had the odd bet down the betting shop. I was at South Harrow Baptist Church at the time and the Baptists were heavily against drinking, heavily against smoking, heavily against betting. And there I was, Sunday School teacher, straight after the service down the pub!

Jesu, Lover of my Soul is our family hymn. It was my father's favourite hymn and it was played at both my father's and my mother's funeral. I had a hard time coming to terms with both the losses, but being a Christian helps that and this hymn is a real celebration of somebody's life. The words are just stunningly moving – it's just a wonderful hymn.'

Rick Wakeman

LEAD KINDLY LIGHT

Lead, kindly Light
amid th'encircling gloom,
Lead thou me on;
The night is dark,
and I am far from home
Lead thou me on.
Keep thou my feet;
I do not ask to see
The distant scene;
one step enough for me.

I was not ever thus,
nor prayed that thou
Should'st lead me on;
I loved to choose
and see my path; but now

Lead thou me on.
I loved the garish day
and, spite of fears,
Pride ruled my will: remember not past years.

So long thy power
hath blest me, sure it still
Will lead me on
O'er moor and fen,
o'er crag and torrent, till
The night is gone,
And with the morn
those angel faces smile,
Which I have loved long since,
 and lost awhile.

'I WAS A DON AT CHRIST CHURCH, OXFORD, where the Jesuit College is only a few yards away, just down the road. The great Jesuit philosopher and theologian Father Martin D'Arcy was in charge there and even non-Catholics, even atheists, respected his intellect. So I began falling under his influence, if you like. At the same time I was working with Communists, so there were a lot of different influences at work in my life.

'I have chosen *Lead Kindly Light* partly for the association with J H Newman. Curiously enough, when I looked at it again, I discovered that it was written in 1833 when he was quite a young man, about 12 years before he became a Catholic. Whereas if you look at it, you'd think it was the story of an old man feeling that he had at last found the faith he should have found much earlier. It's very strengthening in the dark hours.'

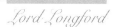

Lord Longford

LEAD KINDLY LIGHT

MINE EYES HAVE SEEN THE GLORY

Mine eyes have seen the glory
of the coming of the Lord.
He is tramping out the vintage
where the grapes of wrath are stored
He has loosed the fateful lightning
of his terrible swift sword.
His truth is marching on.

Glory, glory hallelujah!
Glory, glory hallelujah!
Glory, glory hallelujah!
His truth is marching on.

I have seen him in the watchfires
of a hundred circling camps,
They have gilded him an altar
in the evening dews and damps.
I can read his righteous sentence
by the dim and flaring lamps.
His truth is marching on.

He has sounded forth the trumpet
that shall never sound retreat.
He is sifting out all human hearts
before his judgement seat.
O, be swift my soul to answer him
be jubilant my feet!
Our God is marching on.

In the beauty of the lilies
Christ was born across the sea,
with a glory in his bosom
that transfigures you and me.
As he died to make us holy,
let us live that all be free,
whilst our God is marching on.

'IT'S WONDERFUL WORKING IN AMERICA because Americans are about success whereas, to a great extent, in England success is looked upon as something not quite right. For instance, my mother and father were always a little worried about my success in programmes like *Callan*. They loved it, but at the same time they were a bit embarrassed by it. But in America they praise success. This hymn is the battle hymn of the Republic. One of the most astonishing things is sitting in a church in New York and, just as we all start belting out *Onward Christian Soldiers*, they go hell for leather for *Mine Eyes Have Seen the Glory*. A wonderful sound.'

Edward Woodward

MY SOUL THERE IS A COUNTRY

My soul there is a country
far beyond the stars
where stands a winged sentry
all skilful in the wars

There above noise, and danger
sweet peace sits crowned with smiles
and One born in a manger
commands the beauteous files

He is thy gracious Friend
and – O my soul, awake!
did in pure love descend
to die here for thy sake

If thou canst get but thither
there grows the flower of peace
that Rose that cannot wither
thy fortress and thy ease

Leave then thy foolish ranges
for none can thee secure
but one who never changes
thy God, thy life, thy cure

'THE COUNTRY IN WHICH I WAS BROUGHT UP was New
Zealand, where my father was a doctor and my mother a writer.
They divorced when I was very young and so I was raised in a
predominantly female environment. I thought women ran the world and that
men seemed rather strange creatures, and it was much the same when we
came to England after the war. But then the men drifted back from the war,
took over all the women's work again and drove them back into the home. So
it came as rather a shock to discover that the world was actually male, that
men ran it and that it was seen as the woman's path to stay home and look
after babies.

'I didn't care what men thought of me very much. Especially when it came
to writing, women somehow had the idea that they were dependent upon men
and didn't want to write anything which would displease men. It did not occur
to me that this was what I was expected to do, so I wrote the truth as I saw it.

'I chose *My Soul There is a Country* simply because it was written by a poet
and arranged by Bach. So it's good stuff.'

Fay Weldon

NOW THANK WE ALL OUR GOD

Now thank we all our God,
With hearts and hands and voices
Who wondrous things hath done,
In whom his world rejoices;
Who from our mother's arms
Hath blessed us on our way
With countless gifts of love,
And still is ours today.

O may this bounteous God
Through all our life be near us,
With ever joyful hearts
And blessed peace to cheer us;

And keep us in his grace,
And guide us when perplexed,
And free us from all ills
In this world and the next.

All praise and thanks to God
The Father now be given,
The Son and him who reigns
With them in highest heaven,
The one eternal God,
Whom earth and heav'n adore;
For thus it was, is now,
And shall be evermore.

'I WANTED TO BE A FOOTBALL COMMENTATOR from the age of 11 and I used to cycle to school doing my commentaries as Raymond Glendenning off the radio. I went to Cranbrook, a public school in Kent, where I didn't do particularly well academically because I was spending far too much time on the sports' field. I always felt inferior to the lads from wealthy families who used to pick me up if my grammar wasn't quite right. Sometimes I was treated like the country bumpkin. Now when I go to schools I say that, given my unpromising background, it just shows that if you want to do something badly enough, maybe you can make it happen.

'This hymn goes back to school days and it's the typical end-of-term song we'd sing at church in Cranbrook. It's one of those lovely traditional hymns that you can let rip to and feel better for.'

Brian Moore

O SON OF MAN

O Son of man, our hero
  strong and tender
Whose servants are the brave
  in all the earth
Our living sacrifice to thee we render
Who sharest all our sorrow,
  all our mirth.

Not in our failures only and our sadness
We seek thy presence,
  comforter and friend
O rich man's guest,
  be with us in our gladness
O poor man's mate,
  our lowliest tasks attend!

O SON OF MAN

'I WENT TO GIGGLESWICK SCHOOL IN THE YORKSHIRE DALES where I actually entertained thoughts of becoming a vicar at one stage. When you climb up that steep hill to the school chapel, you do actually feel closer to God because it is so high, and I did think quite seriously that I might follow Holy Orders. I know it's hard to imagine but I was a very thin boy. I was bright academically but very embarrassed to be so thin. The day I scaled six stone was one of the happiest days of my life! Being a weakling, I was no good at sport but in the summer term, if you didn't like cricket, you could do estate work. One of the jobs I did was to build a path up to the chapel, and I'm delighted to say that path still exists. I'm very proud of that path. It wasn't just me – it was a whole team of us – but that path is now part of a little heritage that I bequeathed to the school…

'My other great memory of Giggleswick was being taught English by Russell Harty. He was an inspirational teacher, a human dynamo, whose influence swept through the school like a whole fleet of new brooms. I remember he came back after one Easter holiday and we asked him what he had done. He said: "Oh I went to BBC Television Centre and went to the bar and had a drink with Eric Sykes." We were so impressed that our school teacher had had a drink with Eric Sykes!

'Sadly, my sister Helen died of cancer in 1998. We were very close. Whenever we saw each other I would be the subject of a tongue-lashing – I was too fat, I should have my hair cut – all the things a sister can tell you. She lived every single day until the very last day: entertaining, cooking, looking after the children, doing all the things that she always did. Life and soul of the party. *O Son of Man* was chosen by my nieces and my brother-in-law to be sung at Helen's funeral in Bradford Cathedral. The Cathedral was absolutely full, daffodils outside, spring sunshine… it was a wonderful day.'

Richard Whiteley

MY FAVOURITE HYMNS

PRAISE TO THE LORD, THE ALMIGHTY THE KING OF CREATION

'THE SADDEST THING THAT EVER HAPPENED TO ME was that my dad died a month before I won an Oscar for *Chariots of Fire*. He was at the premiere, but he missed the Oscar ceremony. I didn't know him at all until I was nearly five because he was away in the war – he ran a section of the army film unit – so there was this enormous gap when I met him. It was almost as if I became twice as fond of him. He was a funny and lovely man – the nicest man I've ever met.

'With the exception of my history teacher, Miss Kirkpatrick, none of the teachers at school bothered to attempt to motivate me. I discovered later in life that I've got a very lateral mind. It works in leaps. I think I'm highly imaginative but the school had no capacity to deal with that – it didn't conform to the way they saw teaching. But Miss Kirkpatrick was electrifying. I did very well in history, and it was enough to give me the confidence to know that I wasn't stupid. I think if I'd done badly in everything, I would have conformed to what some of the other teachers felt, which was that I was just dumb.

'I was always interested in films. I was very lucky in that my home in Southgate was within walking distance of four cinemas, so I could see four movies in any given week. I think that did suit my particular level of intelligence and it allowed me to release my imagination. I had a tremendous memory for films and can still remember moments from films I saw in my very early teens.

'*Praise to the Lord, the Almighty the King of Creation* was written by a German pastor in the seventeenth century immediately after the most dreadful plague. What I find extraordinary about it is to try and imagine the devastation – he was writing it in a town that had lost half its inhabitants in the plague – and yet it is such a hopeful hymn with a beautiful tune and beautiful lyrics. You can't leave church having heard this hymn without feeling pretty good about the world and maybe even not too bad about yourself.'

Lord Puttnam

Praise to the Lord,
the Almighty, the King of creation;
O my soul, praise him,
for he is thy health and salvation:
Come, ye who hear,
Brothers and sisters, draw near,
Praise him in glad adoration.

Praise to the Lord,
who o'er all things so wondrously reigneth,
Shelters thee under his wings, yea,
so gently sustaineth:
Hast thou not seen?
All that is needful hath been
Granted in what he ordaineth.

Praise to the Lord,
who doth prosper thy work and
  defend thee;
Surely his goodness and mercy
shall daily attend thee:
Ponder anew
All the Almighty can do,
He who with love doth befriend thee.

Praise to the Lord!
O let all that is in me adore him!
All that hath life and breath
come now with praises before him!
Let the Amen
Sound from his people again:
Gladly for ay we adore him!

PRAISE MY SOUL

Praise my soul, the King of heaven;
To his feet thy tribute bring.
Ransom'd, heal'd, re-stor'd, forgiven,
Who like me his praise should sing?
Praise him! Praise him!
Praise him! Praise him!
Praise the everlasting King.

Praise him for his grace and favour
To our fathers in distress;
Praise him still the same for ever,
Slow to chide, and swift to bless.
Praise him! Praise him!
Glorious in his faithfulness.

Father-like, he tends and spares us;
Well our feeble frame he knows;
In his hands he gently bears us,
Rescues us from all our foes.
Praise him! Praise him!
Widely as his mercy flows.

Angels, help us to adore him;
Ye behold him face to face;
Sun and moon, bow down before him,
Dwellers all in time and space.
Praise him! Praise him!
Praise with us the God of grace.

'WHEN MY WIFE AND I WERE CONFIRMED about four years ago, we were given a choice of hymns and this was one that we both settled on very quickly. It was a tiny service – just the two of us at our local church – but there was a really nice choir and I just remember this particular hymn and thinking the whole thing was quite special. I was 55, my wife was 52, and I felt we were returning to where probably our parents wanted us to be 40 years earlier.'

Lord David Puttnam

'THIS IS ONE OF MY FAVOURITE HYMNS and I like singing it when I'm in church. It is uplifting and very often in my job you need a sense of uplift, particularly after Prime Minister's Question Time!'

Charles Kennedy

THE DAY THOU GAVEST, LORD, IS ENDED

The day thou gavest, Lord, is ended,
The darkness falls at thy behest,
To thee our morning hymns ascended,
Thy praise shall sanctify our rest.

We thank thee that thy Church unsleeping,
While earth rolls onward into light,
Through all the world her watch is keeping,
And rests not now by day or night.

As o'er each continent and island
The dawn leads on another day,
The voice of prayer is never silent,
Nor dies the strain of praise away.

The sun that bids us rest is waking
Our brethren 'neath the western sky,
And hour by hour fresh lips are making
Thy wondrous doings heard on high.

So be it, Lord; thy throne shall never,
Like earth's proud empires, pass away;
The kingdom stands, and grows forever,
Till all thy creatures own thy sway.

'I WAS RECORDING THE ALBUM *SIX WIVES OF HENRY VIII* and we were finishing off the very last track, which was Ann Boleyn. I remember going to bed at about two or three o'clock in the morning but not being able to sleep because I was worried about that piece of music. There was something that was wrong, but I couldn't make it out. Eventually I dropped off to sleep, but it was no more than a semi-sleep. It was a dream and I dreamed about execution. It was one of those bizarrely mixed-up dreams. I was there, so was Henry VIII and so was the boss of A & M Records. It was very vivid, and after the execution everybody around sang *The Day Thou Gavest, Lord, Is Ended*. I can remember in my heart thinking, that's the ending. From that, it's become very much part of my life. I do about 40 musical performances in churches each year and I always close the evening by playing this. And at home I often just sit at the piano and play it before I go to bed. It's a lovely way to finish the day and to say "thank you" for every day. And if there's anybody who should say thank you for being there every day, it's me!'

Rick Wakeman

THE KING OF LOVE MY SHEPHERD IS

The King of love my shepherd is,
Whose goodness faileth never;
I nothing lack if I am his
And he is mine for ever.

In death's dark vale I fear no ill
With thee, dear Lord, beside me
Thy rod and staff my comfort still
Thy cross before to guide me.

And so through all the length of days
Thy goodness faileth never
Good shepherd, may I sing thy praise
Within thy house for ever.

TV AGONY AUNT DENISE ROBERTSON is able to call on her own painful experiences when offering advice to viewers.

'My first husband, Alex, and I lived in a mining community in the north-east. He was the assistant harbour master and I used to go down to the harbour with my child by the hand, the ships would come in and it was so romantic. I started to write and I eventually wrote an award-winning play. In the week that play went out – and there were people coming up from London telling me I had a rosy future – I found out that my husband had a terminal illness. He died six months later.

'I had a child to take care of and a widows' pension of £10 5s a week to keep the two of us, so I think that I battened it all in, I put the lid on my feelings. That is why I am a passionate advocate of counselling now because you ought to let grief go.

'I don't see God as in a sense an entity, I see God as an all-pervading goodness. This hymn says that – "whose goodness faileth never". And it has never failed me. Whatever it is, it has never failed me.'

Denise Robertson

TO JESUS' HEART ALL BURNING

To Jesus' heart, all burning
With fervent love for all,
My heart with fondest yearning
Shall raise its joyful call.
While ages course along,
Blest be with loudest song
The sacred heart of Jesus
By ev'ry heart and tongue
The sacred heart of Jesus
By ev'ry heart and tongue

When life away is flying,
And earth's false glare is done;
Still, Sacred Heart, in dying
I'll say I'm all thine own.
While ages course along,
Blest be with loudest song
The sacred heart of Jesus
By ev'ry heart and tongue.
The sacred heart of Jesus
By ev'ry heart and tongue.

'MY FATHER TAUGHT ME MASS. He knew the priest part and the altar boys' part, and he had me kneeling in the kitchen until my knees were sore. We went to St Joseph's Church in Limerick where he tried to get me in as an altar boy, but they took one look at me and saw that I was obviously from a lane. I was a ragged urchin with the usual scabs on my knees and everything, and the sacristan just closed the door in my face.

'I remember priests, or brothers from foreign missions in Africa, coming into our school and standing in front of the class and saying that we needed to help the little black babies. They'd say: "Tomorrow you have to bring in sixpence." You'd go back to your mother and she'd say: "Go away, I don't have a penny." There were many kids in the class, including us, who couldn't bring in sixpence, and they were humiliated by the master or whatever priest was collecting this money.

'This was one of the hymns of the confraternity which was an institution that all the working classes belonged to, all the unemployed. There were a thousand boys all singing *Jesus' Heart All Burning*. It was one escape from the lanes and the poverty.'

Frank McCourt

THE LORD IS MY SHEPHERD

The Lord is my Shepherd I shall not want,
He makes me to lie down in green pastures,
He leads me beside restful waters
He refreshes my soul,
He guides me in paths of righteousness
for His name's sake.
Even though I walk through the valley of
the shadow of death
I will fear no evil, for You are with me

Your rod and Your staff give me comfort,
You spread your table for me in the sight
of my enemies,
You richly anoint my head with oil;
my cup overflows.
Surely goodness and kindness
will follow me all the days of my life
And I shall live in the Lord's house
for many long years.

'I LIVED WITH MY GRANDMOTHER AS A KID. I was never away from her. Whatever happened to me, I always told her and she was always there for me. I think my faith was really rocked when she died. *The Lord Is My Shepherd* was sung at my gran's funeral. To me, it's about the passing over from one life to another and every time I hear that hymn it brings back great memories of my grandmother.'

Bruce Jones

'I JUST THINK THIS IS A BEAUTIFUL HYMN. It's gentle, it's romantic and it tells a story. I loved it at school and I still do.'

Lord Archer

THE LORD IS MY SHEPHERD

AVE MARIA

Ave Maria

Gratia plena Dominus Tecum

Benedicta tu in

Mulieribus et benedictus fructus ventrie

Tui Jesus sancta Maria

Sancta Maria, Maria

Ora pro nobis

Nobis pecca to ribus nunc et in

Hora in hora mortis nostrae.

Amen.

'*AVE MARIA* BY LESLEY GARRETT WAS VERY SPECIAL. I was asked to work on a BBC programme called *Jobs for the Girls* with Pauline Quirke and Linda Robson. They were completely mad girls and they had to sing *Rule Britannia* in front of a live audience. They had Lesley Garrett to help them and the BBC asked me if I would dress the three of them for this performance. It was a lot of fun and I remember in the rehearsal stepping on the stage at Hampstead Heath thinking, "I want to do this, I want to walk out there and sing *Rule Britannia*." But I said, "I can't, I'm just the frock maker, I should be in the background." Anyway, the show was a great success and I've gone on to make many gowns for Lesley Garrett. She's a great girl.'

David Emmanuel

'I HAD A WONDERFUL CHILDHOOD and a very good relationship with my father who was a gunner in the army in India. He was Irish. He did strange things sometimes. He woke me up at three o'clock one morning. He said: "Son, wake up." I said: "What is it, dad?" He said: "Look, I never shot a tiger." I said: "Why are you telling me?" He said: "I've got to tell somebody."

'*Ave Maria* is very beautiful. My late wife, Paddy, was a soprano and she used to sing it in church. God, it was beautiful.'

Spike Milligan

AVE MARIA

'I WAS BROUGHT UP IN SOUTH AFRICA and we came back to England when I was about 12. I remember *Ave Maria* at the first school I went to in Wiltshire. It was a great sound in the ancient chapel there, and so it sort of stuck and I still like it.'

Sir Ranulph Fiennes

'I WAS A CHOIRBOY IN IRELAND FOR SEVEN YEARS. People think I'm joking, but I actually had quite a good voice – soprano alto tenor. *Ave Maria* was one of the pieces that we used to learn and sing in the choir, and it was always one of those songs that after concerts or church services, people would say: "Wasn't that lovely!" And it is, it always is lovely.'

Eamonn Holmes

Ave Maria! Mater Dei Ora pro nobis
Peccatoribus, Ora, Ora pro nobis,
Ora, Ora pronobis Peccatoribus
Nune et in hora mortis, in

Hora mortis nostrae,
In hora mortis, mortis nostrae, in
Hora mortis nostrae.
Ave Maria

MY FAVOURITE HYMNS

MY FAVOURITE HYMNS

INDEX OF HYMNS

INDEX OF CONTRIBUTORS

ACKNOWLEDGEMENTS

A

Abide with me
Lyte/Monk
All creatures of our God and king
W H Draper (1855–1933)
All hail the power of Jesus' name
Perronet/Schrubsole
All people that on earth do dwell
Old Hundreth
All things bright and beautiful
Alexander/Monk
Amazing grace
John Newton (1725–1807)
Ave Maria
Gounod/Bach and Schubert

B

Be thou my vision
Irish, c. 8th Century
Trans. Mary Bryne (1883–1931)
& Eleonor Hull (1860–1935)

C

Count your blessings
Excell/Oatman

D

Dear Lord and father of mankind
Whittier/Parry

E

Eternal father, strong to save
Whiting/Dykes

F

Faith of our fathers
Sawston/Faber
Fight the good fight
John Samuel Bewley Monsell (1811–1875)

G

Glorious things of thee are spoken
Newton/Haydn
Go down Moses
Harry T Burghleigh
Gracious spirit Holy ghost
Christopher Wordsworth (1807–1885)
based on 1 Corinthians 13; Psalm 68: 13

H

Hail glorious Saint Patrick
Traditional/Sister Agnes
Hail Queen of Heaven
Henry/Lingard
He who would valiant be
Bunyan
How sweet the name of Jesus sounds
Newton/Reinagle

I

Immortal, invisible God only wise
Chalmers Smith

J

Jerusalem
Blake/Parry
Jesu, lover of my soul
Charles Wesley (1707–1788)
Jesus, tender shepherd, hear me
Traditional/Duncan

L

Lead kindly light
J H Newman/Purdy
Love Divine all loves excelling
Wesley/Stainer

M

Mine eyes have seen the glory
Julia Ward Howe (1819–1910)
My soul there is a country

N

Now thank we all our God
Martin Rinkart (1586–1649). Trans.
Catherine Winkwort (1827–1878)

O

Onward Christian soldiers
Sullivan/Baring-Gould
O praise ye the Lord
Henry Williams Baker (1821- 1877)

P

Praise My Soul the King of Heaven
Goss/Lyte
*Praise to the Lord the Almighty the
King of Creation*
Don Herren/Winkworth

S

Soul of my saviour
Traditional/W J Maher
Swing low sweet chariot

T

The Day thou gavest, Lord, has ended
Scholefield/Ellerton
To Jesus' heart all burning
Schlor/Christie
The king of love my shepherd is
Henry Williams Baker (1821–1877)
The Lord is my shepherd
Psalm 23 from 'The Scottish Psalter' (1650)
The passion chorale
Gerhardt/Bach
There is a green hill far away
Horsley/Alexander

W

When wilt thou save the people
Elliott/Somervell
Who would true valour see
Priscilla Jane Owens (1829-1899)